In Grandpa's
Hands

A Child's Celebration of Family

BY MARLENA E. UHRIK, Ed.D.

Illustrations by Barbara Cervone

White Stag Press

ISBN 13: 978-097925835-0

Library of Congress Control Number: 2008924035

Original creative concept: Marlena E. Uhrik, Ed.D.

Senior Designer: Chuck Donald

White Stag Press

a division of

Publishers Design Group, Inc.

Roseville, California

www.publishersdesign.com

1.800.587.6666

Printed in China

For
Grandpa Larry
with
Love

Acknowledgements

It is with deep gratitude that I acknowledge the many people who have contributed to my book, *In Grandpa's Hands*. It has been a great honor that I have been able to work with people who caught the vision and contributed their time, talent, and their heart and soul to the production of this book: my husband, Bill Wheelock, and illustrator, Barbara Cervone. Special thanks go to Lynda Selvig and Kern Toy for their inspiration and hard work in the early stages, and to J Oliver for modeling his little hand.

Last, and certainly not least, deep appreciation goes to my Dad, Larry Blevins for his time, patience, and love. Thank you for modeling your hands for this book—the same hands that plowed farmland, built things of beauty, and held my hand throughout the years. Thank you for the gift of being who you are to our family and generations to come.

About the Author

*T*his prominent children's advocate has received national and international recognition. U.S. Congressman Pete Stark honored her achievements by nominating Dr. Uhrik as a Community Hero for the work she has done in her community. This resulted in her selection as a 1996 Olympic Torch runner. She also served as a member of a U.S. delegation that attended a UNICEF Conference on Early Childhood Education in South Africa.

An untiring community leader, Dr. Uhrik also originated and directed The Kids' Breakfast Club, a non-profit organization that promotes the healthy development of children and their families. Dr. Uhrik has received numerous awards and citations for improving the quality of life for children. Most recently, she was recognized in the US House of Representatives Congressional Record.

Dr. Uhrik has been an educator for 40 years and has a doctorate degree in Educational Leadership. She is currently working as a consultant for the California Department of Education in Sacramento, California. She is married and has two grown children and three grandchildren.

She is the author of several books including *A Guidebook for Family Day Care Providers, The ABC's of Home Improvement,* and *In Grandpa's Hands.*

From the Author

*I*n *Grandpa's Hands* was created as a result of my experience seeing my elderly dad go through a life-threatening surgery. It was the long battle to recovery that had me reflecting on what my dad meant to me and the entire family—his children, grandchildren, and his great grandchildren. Through his struggle to recovery, it became even more apparent who he was, not only to his family, but his friends, and neighbors and the world.

In Grandpa's Hands was written to honor not only this Grandpa, but to honor all Grandpas and who they are to the world. They are the keeper of the family, the strength, the history, and wisdom of generations. They are the ones who teach us the lessons of life through their actions, words, and deeds. Grandpas teach us the things we need to know for everyday life and help carry us into our future.

In Grandpa's Hands is designed to promote discussion about the importance of the elderly and their role in our lives and our society. It is meant to honor the simple things in life that remind us of our gratitude for the people who bring us joy and happiness.

—Dr. Marlena E. Uhrik, June 2008

*I*n Grandpa's
hands there is...
a cup.

*I*n Grandpa's
hands there is...
a diary.

*I*n Grandpa's
hands there is...
a feather.

In Grandpa's hands there is... a trowel.

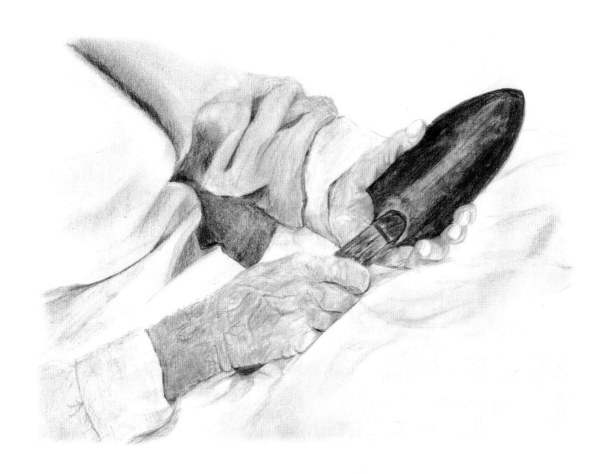

In Grandpa's
hands there is…
a flower.

*I*n Grandpa's
hands there is...
a bird.

*I*n Grandpa's
hands there is...
a starfish.

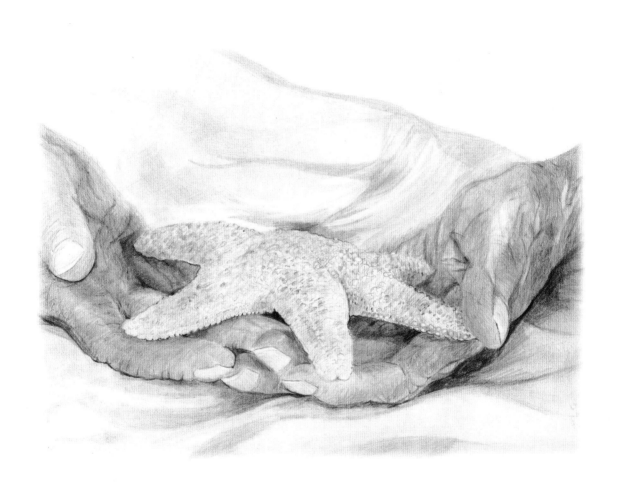

*I*n Grandpa's
hands there is…
a hat.

*I*n Grandpa's
hands there is...
a ball.

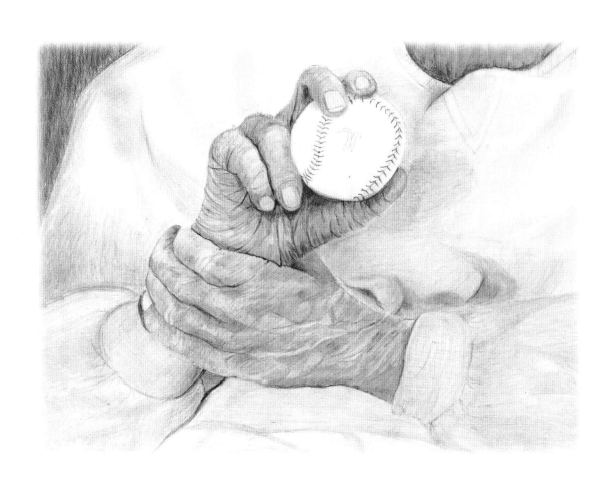

*I*n Grandpa's
hands there is...
an apple.

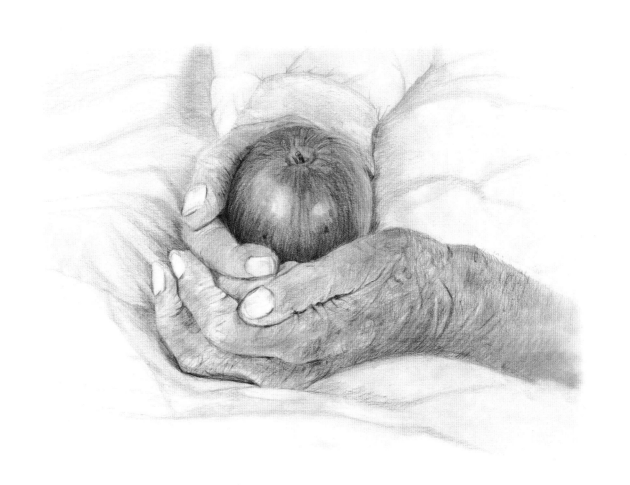

*I*n Grandpa's
hands there is…
a camera.

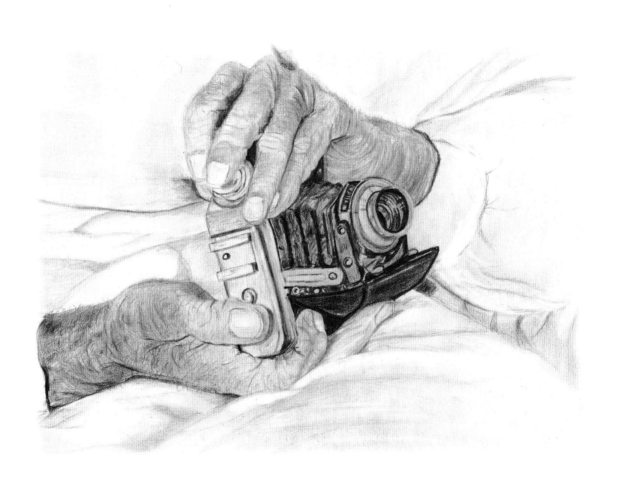

*I*n Grandpa's
hands there is…
mine.

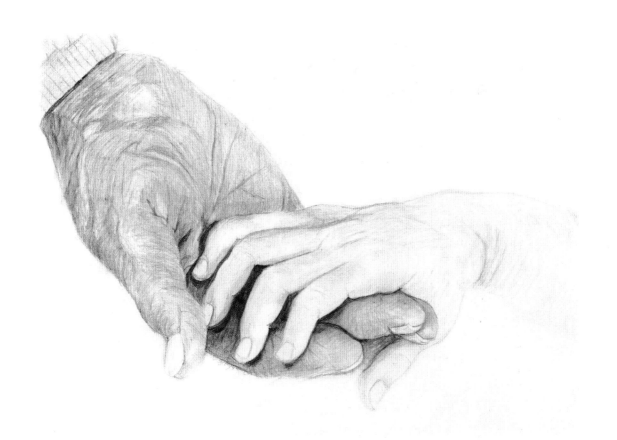

In Grandpa's Hands Resources

Dr. Marlena Uhrik has developed other products that enhance family and multi-generational relationships. Her web site is routinely visited by those looking for new and fresh ideas on family related topics. Please visit it to stay informed about her speaking schedules and writing activities.

Below is a list of a few of the many online resources that focus on generational, kids, and family issues:

www.MyGrandmaAndMe.com

www.TheReadingTub.com

www.GrandKidsAndMe.com

www.gt.pitt.edu/intergenerational_sites.htm

www.intergenugo.org

www.InGrandpasHands.com

www.JustForMom.com

www.MomsChoiceAwards.com

Purchasing copies of *In Grandpa's Hands*

Please purchase copies from your local bookstore or online from Amazon.com. If you are not able to locate a copy, or would like to order other books, calendars, or note cards, please visit *www.InGrandpasHands.com.*

Dr. Uhrik's speaking and writing activities

Dr. Uhrik would love to speak at your next event and is also available for writing articles for organizations that focus on family, parenting, aging, and generational issues. Contact her through email at DrMarlena@InGrandpasHands.com.

Bulk and institutional purchases

For special, bulk discount and school, government, and institutional purchases, please contact the publisher at orders@publishersdesign.com, or call 1.916.784.0500.

Libraries and bookstores

Please order through your trade wholesaler or contact the publisher (Publishers Design Group, Inc.) for distributor information by calling 1.916.784.0500.

"In Grandpa's Hands Note Cards" are a special way for children to let grandpa know how much they appreciate him. Each collection contains twelve cards, each with a different drawing . (Available at *www.InGrandpasHands.com.*)

Check web site for current year's edition.

"In Grandpa's Hands Calendar" makes an excellent decorative addition to any child's room. Featuring the same pencil drawings as those in the book, it is beautiful to look at and is a loving reminder of the relationship between children and their grandpas. (Available at *www.InGrandpasHands.com.*)

White Stag Press
a divison of
Publishers Design Group, Inc.
www.PublishersDesign.com